The FOURTH MYSTERY

Birth & Death

C. G. Harrison

HERMETICA

San Rafael, Ca

Hermetica Press, 2007
First edition, Rider & Co., 1929

For information, address:
Hermetica Press, P.O. Box 151011
San Rafael, California 94915, USA

Library of Congress Cataloging-in-Publication Data

Harrison, C. G., b. 1855.
The fourth mystery : birth and death / C.G. Harrison. — Reprint ed.

p. cm.
Originally published: London : Rider & Co.
ISBN 978-1-59731-209-7 (pbk. : alk. paper)
1. Theosophy. I. Title.
BP565.H37F68 2007
299´.934—dc22   2007027051

"THE FOURTH MYSTERY"

The author of this volume—an independent student, the result of whose investigations extending over a period of many years is embodied in this work—here outlines a system of occultism reminiscent in a marked degree of the Rosicrucian school. His thesis revolves round the central problem of the mystery of birth and death. Neither spiritualism, psychic research, nor theosophy by themselves are sufficient, he contends, to explain this "Fourth Mystery", although the solution suggested by the author involves due ackowledgment and appreciation of each in its degree. The reader will find in this little book a distinctive and interesting contribution to the literature of occultism.

PREFACE

ONE of the chief disadvantages of Occult Science is that, unlike all other kinds of science, it is occult or secret. That this is necessary I should be the last to deny, for certain secrets, if revealed to the public, would dissolve the foundations of Society. Accordingly, everyone who is initiated (after probation) into an occult fraternity is required to take an oath not to reveal anything at all without permission from his superiors; and this for two reasons, (i) because odd pieces of information, especially such as have to do with figures, might give a clue to mathematicians who would make further use of them, and (ii) because the revelation of some secrets would only provoke ridicule among the "profane" scientists. But, in these days, facilities exist for self-initiation, and by a very ancient rule a more learned brother is bound to give information to every initiate who can prove to his satisfaction that his ignorance puts him at a scientific disadvantage. This rule is as old as the days of

PREFACE

Aristotle and accounts for some of his scientific "eccentricities", for he was often unable to make proper use of his information. Usually a self-initiate is left to make his own discoveries but is told whether he is right or wrong. That is my own disadvantage, or, perhaps, on the whole, to my advantage. In dealing with the great mystery of Birth and Death, the fourth of the seven,[1] together with a minor one—that of the Eighth Sphere—I consider myself at liberty to impart to the public everything I deem prudent, without asking permission from anyone.

Perhaps I may here give my own definition of Occult Science, for it is sometimes confounded with occult acts, such as Magic; the difference is as great as the difference between pure and applied mathematics. It is a knowledge of the rules of harmony (reduced to a system) not in relation to the musical scale, but of the spiritual substratum of all physical phenomena which is the region of Cause, for, as the Hindu philosopher Kapila said: "The effect is the unfoldment of the cause in time."

We are surrounded by natural mysteries, the key

[1] i The Abyss. ii Number. iii Affinity. *iv Birth and Death.* v Evil. vi The Word. vii "Godliness". The last is mentioned by St. Paul, μέγα ἐσνὶ το της εὐσεβείας μυστήριον, I Tim. iii, 16.

to which is evolutionary emergence. No one will deny that a philosopher, a musician, an engineer, or a Prime Minister should have his origin in a primitive germ cell just visible in a microscope is as much a mystery as that two gases, oxygen and hydrogen, when chemically combined, should become something so different from each as water. The first stage of man's life is invisible in his mother's womb, and also his last stage is invisible, in the grave. What is the cause of his coming hither and going hence? Where was he before he was born and where is he after he is dead? Few people concern themselves with the former question and are contented with the reply that God created, or brought him into being. But what is interesting nearly everybody now—probably more than ever before the Great War forced the question on so many of us—is what becomes of us after Death? Is there a soul, and is it immortal; or, at least, does it last a reasonable time? Does it concern itself with those who still remain on earth? When we come to die, in our turn, shall we rejoin our friends, and, if so, shall we recognize each other? If a woman of 25 dies, leaving a child of five, and that child should live to be 80, will mother and child recognize each other at the respective ages of 80 and 105?

These and a hundred other questions may be asked, including whether Einstein will have the opportunity of discussing relativity with Newton, or has Saint Joan of Arc already compared ideas with the Grand Inquisitor who condemned her to the stake? Spiritualists, I believe, are prepared with an answer to such questions satisfactory to themselves, but, as I hope to show, to themselves only.

The Disciples on the Mount of Transfiguration are reported to have recognized two dignified figures as Moses and Elias. Doubtless the future state of the departed involves certain mysteries to which even occult science is not prepared to give a solution. Our task is simpler, and restricted to the question: " Where were we ordinary people before we were born, and what becomes of us when we die?" In the following pages an attempt will be made to elucidate this mystery—the Fourth of the Seven Great Mysteries of Occult Science, if not completely, at least partially and to the best of my ability.

A concluding word is necessary. Many think

that religion and science of all kinds are natural enemies like cat and dog, and of occult science perhaps with more reason, seeing that it is often mixed up with necromancy, Buddhism, and generally, with anti-Christian principles and heresies of all kinds. But though it is true that certain occultists have taken what is called the "left-hand path", it is no more true of all than to say every religious man is, *ipso facto*, a hypocrite. The present writer is an Anglo-Catholic and has convinced himself by study that most heresies, and particularly the great historical ones, have arisen from perversion or neglect of fundamental occult truths.

CONTENTS

"THE FOURTH MYSTERY"

CHAPTER I

SPIRITUALISM OR NECROMANCY

THE seven ages of man are familiar to us through Shakespeare, but, though he had got hold of a great truth, he spoilt it, *more suo*, by making it the vehicle of what in those days passed for wit. Man's earth life does not begin as an "infant mewling and puking in his nurse's arms", nor does it end with the expiry of his last breath. It begins and ends with two invisible stages, the womb and the grave, and *both belong to the earth life.* The grave, as we call it, was known to the Jews as *Sheol* or *Hades*, and to the Catholic Church as Purgatory, or Purification from earthly appetites, and both are of the nature of a preparation for a · future state. Shakespeare's seven ages are really only five: infancy, childhood, youth, maturity, and

B

decline, and together with the invisible stages, make up the complement of seven. Now the people who call themselves Spiritualists ignore this last stage, and imagine that they can, through living persons called mediums, communicate with what they call the "spirits" of the deceased which they suppose exist in a disembodied state, or, as St. Paul says, "naked", and yet live in a world very like our own called the "Summer-land".

It is difficult to say why so many people prefer to believe in the heathen doctrine of the immortality of the soul rather than the Christian one of the resurrection of the body, unless it is because the tendency to visualize the unseen leads them to think of the soul as having shape and consequently resembling a more or less unstable human form. In other words, they believe in the survival and persistence of a very unsatisfactory quasi-material body rather than the resurrection of a sensible and solid one. If by the soul is meant the human personality minus the body or vehicle of its activities during earth life, the phenomena of the séance-room afford no evidence of its persistence, far less of its permanence, after that change. That the spirits of the dead do really communicate in this way with the living is, however, firmly believed by a large number of people (some of them quite intelligent and even scientific persons), in spite of occasional fraudulent "mediums" and experiments proving telepathy and the various theories of subconscious thought transference between the living. But even if we admit that the communicating intelligence is in any real sense the deceased person —and there are many reasons for doubting it—the information they give is of such a character as to make it difficult to believe in the continuity for any length of time of such a maimed and unsatisfactory existence.

What is now called Spiritualism was formerly known as necromancy. It is in no sense concerned with life and immortality, but with certain aspects of death or the re-absorption into the world vortex of the forces that went to make up the earth life of the individual. This is, in the nature of things, an *involutionary* process, whereas the resurrection of the body is *evolutionary*, being an increase of life values consequent on a quickening of the spirit by a divine life impulse conveyed through the Sacrament of our Lord's Body and Blood in a

"THE FOURTH MYSTERY"

Christian. As He rose from the dead, so shall we rise by partaking of His life.[1]

One of the first things that strikes us is that these messages from the dead, and accounts of "Summerland", or the regions in which these beings are supposed to live, are fatuous to the point of absurdity, and, what is more to the purpose, they contain not a single idea that was not on the earth before.

Professor Broad[2] examines seventeen theories of so-called spirit control, and, as a result, comes to the conclusion that the least unsatisfactory of them is that one in which what he calls the psychic factor that survives the dissolution of the individual enters temporarily into association with the medium; that upon this association emerges a new mind which is neither that of the medium nor of the deceased but retains some of the characteristics of both. It is suggested that the individual in earth life is the embodiment in matter of an isolated current of universal force or stream of life which, on his

---

[1] It should be clearly understood that this is what is called in theological language a "covenanted mercy of God" as distinguished from the "uncovenanted" mercy which would apply to a righteous Jew or heathen. The Church has long outgrown the opinion of Augustin that the death of the body destroys, *ipso facto*, the covenanted mercy. See also 1 Cor. xv, 29.

[2] The Mind and its Place in Nature.

death reverts to the main stream. But the return need not take place immediately. We may even imagine some degree of recalcitrance, an eager clinging to earth life, and a readiness to combine with a medium or other person who will give him the opportunity of quenching his thirst for material enjoyment at unwholesome springs. It is this new mind that is a product of the combination between the two and invents the spirit messages.

Distinction between body and spirit belongs to a metaphysical theory which has filtered down into popular thought, and got itself fixed in popular phraseology. Whether it be sound or not, to speak of this world and another is a theory and not a basic fact. What stands in the evidence is that things exist where they are, not how they got there, which is a theory. In past ages the sun was said to go away at night and return in the morning. Even survival was held to account for the strange doings of the sun. May it not be that we are in the presence of a similar problem? If so, it will react upon the whole body of our knowledge as every new discovery inevitably does. Its effect on knowledge might even be revolutionary. We know that people are born and die, but do we know anything

more than that they appear and disappear like the
sun? The spirits of the séance-room talk of "he"
and "she", of yesterday, to-morrow, next year, etc.,
distinctions that refer to astronomical conditions,
and would be meaningless without them. All this
suggests that they and we stand on a common
biological ground, and since biological facts, like
all others are not isolated, we should be able from
one fact alone to build a whole system to corres-
pond, as Owen was able to construct from a single
bone the whole fossil skeleton of an extinct
reptile.[1]

If to be really dead is to sever finally our connection with this world of sense, the first thing
is to inquire whether these spirits or ghosts who are
said to communicate with the living are in that
condition, or merely undergoing the seventh or last
stage in the seven ages of man. It must be remembered that the Society for Psychical Research has
established beyond question that phantasms of the
living bear to phantasms of the dead somewhere
about the proportion of 20 of the former to one
of the latter; and, moreover, that it has been found

[1] See Presidential Address before the S.P.R. for 1917, by L. P.
Jacks.

much easier to get into communication with the comparatively recently departed than with the "spirits" of Shakespeare, Luther, etc., communications from whom even the Spiritualists themselves regard as extremely unsatisfactory, tainted with suspicion, or even spurious.

CHAPTER II

THE THEOSOPHISTS

IN 1894 I published a course of lectures, delivered before the Berean Society, of which I was President for that year, under the title of "The Transcendental Universe". Reading them again in 1929, I find nothing of importance to revise and little, except one or two details, to correct.[1] The object of the lectures was to confute certain false teachings for which the late Madame Blavatsky was responsible in her monumental work, "The Secret Doctrine" (Vols. I & II only; Vol. III is worthless). It appears that such occult science as Mme. Blavatsky undoubtedly possessed died with her, and the Theosophists of the later period have been mainly occupied in raising imposing edifices of bricks without the occult scientific mortar required for binding them together.

---

[1] The "severe blow" on p. 31, it seems, was directed not against Spiritualism but the Theosophical Society, and the claim of Mr. W. Q. Judge to have had direct correspondence with the Masters on Mahatmas. Also, on p. 32, I was mistaken in giving Vienna as the scene of the Congress of European and American occult fraternities. It was not Vienna but another important city on the Danube.

THE THEOSOPHISTS

In the Transcendental Universe, mention was made of the Seven Great Mysteries of Occult Science, the penetration of which is the path to wisdom. With these, Madame Blavatsky was probably acquainted, though she studied them in their wrong order, having been initiated into them irregularly; and in regard to Mystery IV (Birth and Death) she made extraordinary mistakes in her "Secret Doctrine". Moreover, in regard to Mrs. Besant, her pupil and successor, she exercised what theologians call a wise and laudable "economy", with the consequence that no theosophist has been able to throw any satisfactory light on Mystery IV, it having never occurred to them to connect it with the "planetary chain" on which the evolution of man is said to take place. This is unfortunate, for they are obliged to rely on "Devachanic" visions, in other words, their own imagination, instead of scientific facts based on genuine occult knowledge.

Since the death of Mme. Blavatsky, in 1891, enormous strides have been made in "profane" science which, it is only fair to say, have done nothing to invalidate the occult knowledge displayed (however perversely) in her "Secret Doctrine". The discovery of the nature of the atom as a vortex of pure force on the physical plane, and the establishment of Relativity and the fourth (or Time-Space) dimension as the acknowledged solution of various scientific problems; all this has revolutionized former conceptions of the universe held in the Nineteenth Century. Matter is no longer thought of as the cause of spirit, but both rather as the two poles of a sphere. The data of our experience are complex things and admit of being analysed. Matter is ultimate in analysis. But they also admit of being built up into a higher synthesis. Pure matter and pure spirit are not experiences but *ideals*; both are ends beyond the reach of human thought, as infinity and zero are present in every finite measure. The most ultimate of all ultimates is Being and Non-Being. The ideal goal of analysis is not the electron, but pure *potentiality*, which is actually null and void. Turning to the other pole of spirit, we can only guess at God, or Pure Being, by looking upwards from our own level of spirituality. We can never *know* but approach towards the Infinite by building up a higher and higher synthesis indefinitely. The empirical finite is the meeting-place of the counter-infinities of being and non-being. They meet to struggle, and the ferment of their energies is what we know as life.[1]

Life, though itself non-material, wherever it exists shows itself through matter as its invariable accompaniment. In favour of this view is the growing inability of science to draw any dividing line between living and non-living matter. Plants, we know, possess life, and it has been shown that even metals respond to stimulus, are subject to fatigue, and react to poison in a manner which is different in degree but not in kind from the behaviour of organisms which are generally regarded as living. Is it not possible, or even likely, that it lurks in all the seven kingdoms of Nature; even the so-called elemental kingdoms below the mineral where our instruments are not sufficiently delicate or precise to detect it?

Life, having once appeared, by the law of its being must evolve, and *its evolution takes the form of emergence.* What is meant by this? Let us

---

[1] I am indebted for these ideas to Mr. Edmond Holmes in an article entitled "A Last Guess at Truth", which appeared in the *Hibbert Journal* for April, 1927.

suppose we combine the two elements oxygen and hydrogen in a certain proportion, and the result is water. Now water exhibits certain characteristics which are not those of either hydrogen or oxygen. They are new in the sense that they are not present in, and could not be deduced from an examination of either constituent of water. In other words, we cannot give a complete account of water in terms of the ingredients of which it is composed.

Everything we are accustomed to call an organic whole arises from emergence—whether a live human being or a Bach's fugue, which has a unity that is quite independent of the notes of which it is composed. When faced with the question: How does life develop; how does it exhibit powers and qualities which were not present at any previous stage in its history? the answer is *Emergence*. Any given power or capacity at which qualities and powers manifest that were not found at preceding life levels is an emerged product.

Now let us, as an aid to mental visualization, assume that the seven globes which go to make up the terrestrial chain are visible and material, instead of being only centres of attraction for the evolution of the kingdoms of Nature. Then globes *a, b*, and *c* are preparatory to, and in a sense the cause of, *d*, our material and visible earth, for, as Mme. Blavatsky admits, they go into pralaya, or cease to manifest, when *d* comes into existence and has cooled down sufficiently to support life. The archetypal forms of the animal, plant and mineral kingdoms are ready for emergence on the higher plane of material existence and will give rise to the birth of a potentially higher kingdom than the animal; for, though the animals will be born on globe *d*, they will not progress to globe *e* until the law of acceleration comes into operation by the passing of the higher away from the chain; for the terrestrial is linked with another planetary chain under a new principality (this time) of Light, when the works of the present prince of darkness are finally destroyed and absorbed into the Eighth Sphere. But this is to anticipate.

To return then, the first of the seven stages of man's earth life is intra-uterine, and in pursuance of the principle that ontogeny is a copy of phylogeny, man goes through the whole course of evolution from mineral to human being in the nine months which elapse from conception to parturition. This is well known to physiologists, and some day the process may be exhibited on the screen of the cinematograph.[1] During this period man evolves the apparatus which enables him to adapt himself to his new conditions, sight, hearing etc.; and by the time he is ready to be born his senses are complete and he enters on his five *visible* stages of earth life. It is in the course of these five stages that man develops what the Theosophists call *Karma*. This and its complementary doctrine of re-incarnation were taken over, not from Buddhism but from the old Hindu religion which existed centuries before Sakya Muni was born but which he adopted and elaborated in his "Path" to wisdom. It is not part of the Christian Revelation, but it has a philosophical interest for all students of comparative religion, and may contain certain elements of truth; though whether, as a Mahatma is reported to have written to Mr. Sinnett, [2] the problem of 777 incarnations is worth while trying to solve is very doubtful. It reminds one of the proverbial blind man searching at night in a dark cellar for a black cat who is not there (or let us say, may not be there).

---

[1] This has been done already in the case of the common domestic fowl, when the period of incubation is only 21 days.

[2] "Secret Doctrine", Vol. I, p. 168.

THE THEOSOPHISTS

Much has been written in favour of the reasonableness of re-incarnation and its automatic provision of strict justice in rewards and punishments for deeds done in the body. At any rate, it appeals to modern thought more strongly than the belief held in the last generation that either eternal bliss or eternal tortures await immediately the expiry of the last breath. Our Lord was so occupied in founding the Kingdom of Heaven on Earth *that we might have life* that He said very little about the state after death with one notable exception: the parable of the rich man and Lazarus, which is a variant of the story of the half-way house on the peak of Chimborazo.[1] It has been deprived of its meaning by the translators of the Authorized Version, who rendered *sheol* or *Hades* by "Hell", implying that the rich man was tortured by the pangs of thirst for ever and ever. There is one reference to re-incarnation which He promptly denied in the particular case of the man who was born blind.

---

[1] The ascending traveller from the sub-tropical valley at the foot is shivering with cold, while the descending traveller from the frost and snow at the summit is complaining of the heat, though the air is at the same temperature for both.

Whether there be anything corresponding to re-incarnation apart from the resurrection of the body at the last day, may or may not be true, but it forms no part of the Christian Faith and may be relegated to the category of philosophical speculation.

Fortunately, the question of how many times we are born and how many times we die is not immediately involved in the mystery of any single birth or death on which I hope to throw some light from the point of view of occult science.

According to theosophical doctrine, the dis-embodied human spirit (if there be such a thing) having worked out his or her Karma on an imaginary ideal plane of existence called "Devachan" (or Avitchi, as the case may be—good Karma in the former and evil Karma in the latter) is impelled to generate more. He is, therefore, thrown back into the vortex of a new terrestrial evolution and is ready in a longer or shorter period for re-incarnation by generating a new *Karma rupa* or principle of desire for material enjoyment.

This, however, is not the teaching of the Tibetan Buddhists; though "Devachan" is a Tibetan word, unlike most of the theosophical terms which are

Indian. Schlagintweit, who was the great authority on Tibet in the Nineteenth Century, says that return from Devachan is impossible and regards it as a kind of ante-chamber to Nirvana. A Tibetan Devachanee, according to Schlagintweit, is a live saint (or Arhat) enjoying in a body, weakened by asceticism, a foretaste of Nirvana which he hopes to attain after death. But this is by the way.

Life, as we have seen, is inseparable from matter, though of course matter may range from the grossest to the most tenuous forms. Even the elementals (or nature souls) have a body of some kind. The blood evocations used by those who practice evil acts are for the purpose of drawing them down to and attaching them temporarily to the material earth and making them thus subserve the nefarious ends of the sorcerer. But we fear that the personal revelations of life in Devachan, communicated to Mr. Stead's "Borderland" in the 1890's, must be relegated to the category of moonshine. Here, however, we are trenching on the subject of what happens after death before explaining why we got from what we have called globe c to our earth which we call globe d.

"THE FOURTH MYSTERY"

The passage from *c* to *d* is of the greatest importance. The invisible intra-uterine period is a preparation of nine months (or thereabouts) for a period of struggle with more or less adverse conditions which may last for many years, and it is during this struggle that character (or Karma) develops. The periods of infancy and childhood, which last much longer in man than the lower animals, require protection and training for the serious business of life. Among barbarous tribes and peoples this takes the form of war in which children engage at a much earlier age than among civilized races. In the latter, commerce, industry, finance (or the art of exploiting our fellow-men), science, the fine arts, and the various human activities we associate with civilization begin with youth, sometimes without much training (or even in the teeth of opposition) and are carried on with greater or less success into the period of decline, and often until death puts a stop to them. It is the aggregate of these activities which determine the qualities of the human being, qualities that are carried over when the individual passes on to globe *e*. From a cosmogenical point of view, the Mystery of Birth and Death are not two but one.

The one cannot be known without the other: it is the obverse and reverse of the medal.

Life on this planet has been called our period of probation, and if it is the hardest part of our probation it is because the course of evolution is so slow. But, though the law of acceleration has now come into play, it must be remembered that we Europeans of the Twentieth Century are not separated from palæolithic man by more than five hundred generations, counting a generation as thirty years. Human sacrifice to propitiate their deities was practised by the Aztecs five hundred years ago, and in our own island before the landing of the Romans, little more than a generation before the Christian era. Further, there is a constant throw back to the fierceness of our ancestors in times of war and revolution. Witness the barbarous murder of the Tsar of Russia and his family in quite recent times.

For modern Europe the process of acceleration did not begin until the Eleventh Century, and, though noticeable in the Middle Ages for those who have eyes to see, it was not until the Sixteenth Century that modern Europe took the first step to becoming really civilized; and from that time

to this it has witnessed a series of throw backs, from
the Thirty Years' War in the Seventeenth Century,
the French Revolution in the Eighteenth, and
the Great War in the Twentieth Century. For
the world generally we may say that, in spite of
various prophets and reformers of religion, the law
of retardation in respect to the evolution of the
highest kingdom of nature—man, prevailed until
the Advent of Jesus Christ, and that of acceleration began when He announced that He saw "Satan
as lightning fall from Heaven".

The distressing slowness of evolution on this
planet is owing to divided allegiance between its
true "Rector" and the usurping Prince of this
world.[1]

So far, I think we may claim to have established
in the light of evolution on the planetary chain
which happens when a baby is born into the world.
We now proceed to inquire into what happens
when a man appears to die and ceases to be visible
because he is put under ground, where his body
decays and is resolved into its mineral constituents.

[1] In occult science the name Rector is applied to to the angelic
intelligence which presides over the course of evolution in every
planet of the Solar System; not only the ones visible to the eye or
the telescope, but that far greater number which are invisible to man
as he is at present constituted.

CHAPTER III

ALL orthodox Theosophists are acquainted with the theory of rings and rounds, of the seven planets and man's progress around them. As a help to mental visualization, this explanation has its merits, but it is often forgotten that the course of evolution is not a *space* but a *time* circle or sphere. Now we are accustomed to think of time in one dimension. A square, cubic, or spherical minute is meaningless to most European thinkers, if we except certain German and Italian mathematicians. It is admitted that even Einstein's Fourth (or Time-space) dimension cannot be made intelligible to those whose studies have not included the higher mathematics. The equations that prove his theory are for most people information in a foreign language they have not learned.

A book which has recently appeared, called "An Experiment with Time",[1] may do something to

---

[1] "An Experiment with Time", by J. W. Dunne. A. & C. Black, Ltd., London, 1929.

familiarize the ordinary man with what the author calls "Serialism" as a multi-dimensional theory of time applied to prophetic dreams, but Mr. Dunne's mathematics are not equal to the task of proving it, which requires an Eddington to develop into a true scientific theory, as Clerk Maxwell proved the non-mathematical Faraday's discovery of electromagnetism.

Accordingly, when the "Secret Doctrine" teaches that the earth and the moon are at the bottom of a vortex of which the spirals are made up of seven globes, and the whole called the terrestrial chain, the ordinary reader gets impatient and throws the book aside, though the faithful swallow it without even a grimace. The "Secret Doctrine" is indeed a kind of revelation of how evolution works, but H.P.B.'s interpretation of the facts is often quite fanciful and, in many places, open to serious criticism. However, let us accept the terrestrial chain with its seven globes in alternate states of *manvantara* and *pralaya*, providing that we rightly understand that the only visible ones are the earth and the moon, and the others not even gaseous, or of a kind that are discoverable by even the most powerful telescopes. It may be convenient to speak of these in their order as *globes a, b, c,* etc., so long as it is understood that they are globes only in a "Pickwickian" sense. Here, again, the matter is still further complicated by a minor mystery of Mystery IV—the mystery of the Eighth Sphere—the right comprehension of which is necessary to the penetration of the Great Mystery of Birth and Death. It is indeed the mystery of eternal death, but we are not now concerned with it, as it will not be fully revealed until the Judgement Day as the mystery of *Involution* as distinguished from evolution which we are now about to examine. Of the terrestrial chain of which our earth is nearly at the bottom of the vortex, the earth may be called globe *d,* the course of evolution proceeding in order from *a, b* and *c* to *d,* and afterwards to *e, f* and *g.* Another thing important to remember is that the terrestrial chain includes the whole seven kingdoms of Nature, and that evolution proceeds on it in accordance with the law of acceleration and retardation.[1]

It is in the course of man's evolution on globe *d,*

---

[1] The law of acceleration and retardation may be thus stated. All evolution is cyclic, in time or space. During the first half of each cycle its rate is subject to a serial diminution, which, if the initial velocity be represented by x, culminates in $\frac{x}{7}$. It then

the earth, that he acquires the gift of language, and this does not begin until he arrives at the third stage, childhood. Instinct, which he has in common with the lower kingdoms of Nature, begins at birth. According to Bergson, language is the medium between instinct and reason, but it is a very imperfect medium for expressing thought, and will require at some future stage to be superseded by some other kind of symbolism. Instinct, on the other hand, carries on the work of evolution in the lower kingdom quite independently of reason and at a very low stage of consciousness. When the implement to be used is organized by Nature, the material furnished by Nature and the result to be obtained willed by Nature, there is little left to choice. When the horse-fly lays its eggs on the legs or shoulders of a horse, it acts as if it knew that its larva has to develop in the horse's stomach, and that the horse in licking itself will convey the larva into its digestive track. When a paralysing wasp stings its victim on just those points where the

increases at the same rate that it diminished, its final corresponding with its initial velocity, the whole series being expressed in multiples of seven. As there are seven kingdoms of Nature, the calculation becomes very complicated when we remember that each in its turn is alternatively in *manvantara* and *pralaya*.

nervous centres lie, so as to render it motionless without killing it, it acts like a learned entomologist and a skilful surgeon rolled into one. The oft-quoted story of the little beetle, the Sitaris, which lays its eggs at the entrance of the underground passages dug by the Anthrophora bee, is a yet more astonishing instance of the elaborate scheme taken by Nature to ensure the reproduction of this beetle whose consciousness is of such a low order as to be almost automatic. Compare these with the instinct that makes the new-born babe seek its mother's breast which it has never seen, and yet about two years later when he hears an epithet applied to a substantive he will immediately understand what it means. The same may be said of the general relation expressed by the verb to the object. Later still, the schoolboy who knows that the master is about to dictate a fraction to him will draw a line before he knows what the numerator and the denominator are going to be. To a certain extent the higher animals have developed this intelligence. The difference between a dog and a Sitaris beetle is enormous. He understands as well as a child the expression: "Naughty dog", but who would say: " Naughty Sitaris " and expect the creature to alter its habits, or even hear the words, much less understand them?

If instinct is the faculty of using an organized natural instrument it is therefore the innate knowledge of a thing. But intelligence is the faculty of constructing unorganized, i.e., artificial, instruments. When Nature gives up endowing a living being with the instrument that may serve it, she endows him with intelligence to see the way out of a difficulty in any circumstances, and find out what is most suitable. According to Bergson, the intellect alone is unable to solve the problem of life. It requires to be supplemented by the faculty of intuition. Some of the greatest discoveries in science, e.g., the discovery of electro-magnetism by Faraday, were believed in before they were proved.[1] Now, in occult science, discoveries of the utmost importance are made, and, to a limited extent, imparted by the exercise of this very faculty of intuition, which is only another way of saying that the *deductive* method is used for discovery and the *inductive* for proof. When an occultist or student of the mysteries is challenged by an exoteric

---

[1] See opposite page.

scientist to give reasons for believing in certain
scientific heresies (e.g., that the law of gravitation
is not universal but applies only to certain distances,
or that there exist somewhere in the solar system
intelligent beings like men, with brains but lacking
skulls whose places are supplied with a law of
adjustment called thermal equilibrium), he can only
answer that, though he believes it, he cannot supply
any proof that the scientist would admit, and, moreover, only lay himself open to rebuke from the
masters of occult science for "throwing pearls
before swine". This is one of the penalties of being
unattached to any recognized occult fraternity. It
is not to say that occult secrets are really incapable
of (inductive) proof or would not yield it to suitable
equations, but in every fraternity secrets of *number*
are the most sacred, and more jealously guarded
than almost any other. To reveal a mathematical
secret in order to satisfy "profane" curiosity would
entail immediate expulsion and perhaps occult
"imprisonment", such as was inflicted on Mme.
Blavatsky.[1] Intuition, says Bergson, is a lamp
. . . almost extinguished, but it glimmers wherever
a vital interest is at stake. On our personality, on

---

[1] See "The Transcendental Universe", p. 36.

our liberty, on the place we occupy in the whole of nature, on our origin and perhaps also on our destiny, it throws a light feeble and vacillating, but which none the less pierces the darkness of the night in which the *intellect* leaves us.[1]

The great error of the doctrines on the spirit has been the idea that by isolating the spiritual life, by suspending it as high as possible above the earth, they were thereby placing it beyond attack; as if they were not thereby simply exposing it to be taken as an effect of mirage. . . . When a strong instinct assures the probability of personal survival they are right not to close their ears to its voice. . . . If there exist "souls" capable of an independent life, whence do they come? When, how, and why do they enter into this body which we see arise, quite naturally, from a mixed cell derived from the bodies of its two parents? All these questions will remain unanswered, a philosophy of intuition will be a negation of science if it does not resolve to see the body *just where it really is*, on the road that leads to the life of the spirit. . . . The matter that it bears along with it, and in the interstices of

---

[1] " Creative Evolution." Authorized Translation, p. 182. Macmillan, 1912.

which it inserts itself, alone can divide it into dis-
tinct individualities. On flows the current, running
through human generations, subdividing itself into
individuals. This subdivision was vaguely indicated
in it, but could not have been made clear without
matter. . . . As the smallest grain of dust is
bound up with our entire solar system, drawn along
with it in that undivided movement of descent
which is materiality itself, so all organized beings,
from the humblest to the highest, from the first
origins of life to the time in which we are, and in
all places as in all times, do but evidence a single
impulsion, the inverse of the movement of matter,
and in itself indivisible. All the living hold
together, and all yield to the same tremendous push.
The animal takes its stand on the plant, man
bestrides animality, and the whole of humanity,
in space and in time, is one immense army gallop-
ing beside and before and behind each of us in
an overwhelming charge, able to beat down every
resistance and clear the most formidable obstacles,
perhaps even death.[1]

---

[1] Ibid., p. 286.

CHAPTER IV

EVOLUTION AND HUMAN SPEECH

WE claim to have established, so far, that instinct, or intuition, is an essential element in evolution, not only in the lower kingdoms of Nature, but of the highest, man, in the first stages of earth life; that it persists throughout that life and is responsible for the antinomy between what we call our higher and lower nature. But, though in the lower animals instinct leads to cruelty and abominations of every kind, in man it is kept in check by the reason and intelligence and, from some of the worst effects, by conscience, of which only a select few of the highest animals have developed even the rudiments. Moreover, the supersession of instinct by reason, though it has modified its worst effects, has produced evils of its own. By means of language, which is its special instrument, or organ, for establishing relations with our fellows, it has conduced to intellectual progress, and at the same time it has been a hindrance to that progress in many ways.

For, though instinct is an almost infallible guide in the very narrow range of the activities displayed by the brute creation, reason is often at a great disadvantage in its own special sphere. Language has been cynically described by a diplomatist (Talleyrand, we think) as an instrument for concealing our thoughts, and, even where the concealment is not wilful, it often lends itself to unconscious deception. Political deception has become a scandal and a byword, and even philosophy and hasty dogmatism in science, art and religion have produced some of the worst consequences. In spite of the enormous advantages which speech gives to man over the lower kingdoms of Nature, it may be doubted whether, as Bergson hints in more than one place, the faculty may not have disadvantages which may be placed to its debit and the consequent credit of the earlier evolved faculty of intuition. It is essentially symbolic, and in future ages may give place to symbolism of another kind better adapted for communication with our fellow-men and also with the higher intelligences that preside over his destiny. A philosophy, says Professor A. N. Whitehead, supplies a spiritual basis for intellectual ideas which takes long to materialize in the form of art. It builds cathedrals before the workmen have moved a stone and it destroys them before the elements have worn down their arches. . . . Thoughts lie dormant for ages, and then, almost suddenly as it were, mankind finds that they have embodied themselves in institutions.[1]

The barbarians who overran Western civilization in Century V did not produce Gothic cathedrals until Century XIII. In Century XVI the religion which had produced them had undergone a profound change, and the spiritual foundation was laid for the science of the Nineteenth Century, which produced, not cathedrals, but the spectroscope. In the preceding century Newton and Leibnitz inaugurated the era of modern mathematics, thus abolishing language as the medium of *exact* thought, which, I believe, in the not very remote future, will take the place in theology of substituting for language the symbolism known as sacramentalism which lies at the root of Catholic Christianity. Accordingly, Centuries XXI or XXII may produce great works of science comparable to the great works of art in the Middle Ages. They may even take the form of some hitherto unimagin-

---

[1] Preface to "Science and the Modern World".

able machine for turning out the finished product of thought, as we turn out the finished product of cloth from the raw wool.

Now, considering that speech and language is such a very imperfect medium for self-expression on this earth, is there any reason for supposing it will exist in the world of superphysical concepts that will succeed this earth's experience, or that the seventh and last stage of earthly life, which is heralded by the death of the body and its conceal-ment in the grave, as in the first it was concealed in the womb, can be anything else than a prepara-tion for a future existence in which a totally different kind of body will have to play its part? It is true that necromancy, or spiritualism, may hinder its progress for a time by keeping the soul earth-bound, but it will escape sooner or later. The present writer recollects a famous materialized spirit, called Katie King, who, after appearing at numerous séances for some years in England and America, took a solemn farewell of her sitters, say-ing that she was about to be translated to "higher spheres". Even Raymond, the son of Sir Oliver Lodge, who contrives to keep in touch with his father and friends of his earth life, seems to have had considerable difficulty in establishing communications with the "spirit" of the much-longer deceased F. W. H. Myers, who can only express himself in rather remote classical allusions, of which he has managed to retain certain reminiscences, and uses them to prove to Sir Oliver that he is still alive, but experiences difficulties in expressing himself which he cannot properly explain.

CHAPTER V

WHEN WE AWAKE

For in that sleep of death what dreams may come?
—SHAKESPEARE.

FROM the point of view we have been examining, man is so deeply sunk in animality as hardly to deserve the title of an intellectual being. Even the rational activity of which he is so proud is a distinctively animal form of intellect where the higher intelligence is veiled and impeded by the conditions of time and space. On the other hand, man occupies a unique position in the universe because he is the lowest of all spiritual beings. He is at the point where the world of spirit touches the world of sense, and it is through and in him that the material creation attains to intelligibility and becomes enlightened and spiritualized. Since he cannot free himself by transcending the conditions of his nature in an intellectual approach to the world of spirit, the Divine Word has manifested Himself to man through the sensible and concrete appropriate to his limitations. Thus the Incarnation does not destroy or supersede Nature. It is analogous and complementary to it, since it restores and extends man's natural function as the bond of union between the material and spiritual phases of existence.[1]

Against the Oriental religions, with their tendency to deny the importance of the body and the reality or value of the material world, Christianity had maintained undeviatingly the dignity of human nature. Up to the time of Aquinas, however, Christian thought had not fully realized the implications of this doctrine. It was perceived by the Arab thinker, Al Ghazzali, who wrote a book called "The Destruction of the Philosophers" (translated into the degenerate Latin of the Tenth Century), not because he was a mere obscurantist, but because he saw more clearly than his opponents the fundamental incompatibility of the central doctrine of Mohammedanism with the clarity of the Hellenic conception of a cosmos. It was the work of the new philosophy known as the Scholastic, and first represented by Aquinas,

---

[1] "Progress and Religion", Christopher Dawson, pp. 174-5. Sheed and Ward, 1929.

to break with the old-established tradition of Oriental spiritualism and neo-Platonic idealism. He taught that man cannot attain in this life to the direct knowledge of spiritual reality. He must build up an intelligible world slowly and painfully from the data of the senses ordered and systematized by science, until at last the intelligible order which is inherent in created things is disengaged from the envelope of matter and contemplated in its relation to God by the light of the *newly-born intelligence* in the spiritual world or Heaven. The *Summa* of St. Thomas Aquinas is an admirable piece of reasoning from the point of view of thirteenth-century science, and as close as Euclid's Geometry. The Church had no doubt that Thomas was a saint. They applied a simple test, and found that, however impartial his summing-up, the verdict was always in the Church's favour. At Rome he is still thought of in the XX Century as having said the last word on all points of dispute between religion and science. "Scholasticism," said Harnack, "is nothing else but scientific thought. Its weakness in the sphere of natural science is simply due to the fact that there was, as yet, no body of observed facts upon which it could exercise itself. Greek science, as embodied in the science of Aristotle, represented a level of scientific achievement far higher than anything which the medieval world could attain to, by its own unaided powers, and it was taken over consequently *en bloc* by the scholastic movement. The science of the Middle Ages," he adds, " exhibits an energy in subjecting all that is real and valuable in the thought of that day to which, perhaps, we can find no parallel in any other age."[1]

Modern science owes its birth to the union of the creative genius of the Renaissance Art as exemplified in Leonardo da Vinci with the mathematical idealism of Plato's metaphysics. But it would seem to follow that if the universe is conceived as a close mechanical order governed by mathematical laws, then man himself is nothing but a by-product of the vast mechanical order revealed by modern science. It could no longer be integrated with the material universe in a single order of reality except by adopting the Cartesian dualism of the *res extensa* and the *res cogitans*.

If neither the Scholasticism of St. Thomas nor

---

[1] "History of Dogma", Adolf Harnack (English translation), Vol. VI, p. 25.

the dualism of Des Cartes can furnish a unified philosophy of matter and spirit, in what direction shall we look for it? The answer must be: " In occult science," which can alone give a rational account of how man evolves into matter and out of it again; and not only man, but the process applies to all the seven kingdoms of Nature; in other words, wherever life manifests itself as a perceptual phenomenon. The Mystery of Birth and Death, in particular, is a unification of the philosophy of spirit and matter.

If we may continue to use the clumsy term "globe", what happens when a man passes from globe d to globe e? For that they do touch whenever a person dies, though in a very different sense, alleged by the frequenters of the séance-room, is implied in the Apostles' Creed. The Holy Ghost, the Holy Catholic Church and the Communion of Saints are linked together with the forgiveness of sins and the life everlasting. But it may be said that large numbers, if not the majority, of those who die are not Christians. That may be, but there is no reason to think that after death they may not become so. Religion is natural to man, and if the world is not Christian it is the fault of Christians who have made their religion odious instead of attractive. In this they have been assisted by the Prince of this World, who is the usurping Rector of the planet Earth, and whose works are destined to be, in the fullness of time, utterly destroyed. It is true that he will endeavour to recruit his shattered and defeated forces on globe *e*, though with little hope of success in the new conditions. The supersession of speech and writing by a better medium of communication will deprive the Father of lies of the weapons he has used here on earth to deceive the nations of the world. Here, however, we are anticipating a phenomenon of which we will treat later, viz., the actual visible contact of what we have agreed to call globes *d* and *e* symbolized in the Apocalypse as the descent of the Holy City to earth and the final triumph of its lawful Prince.

But we must return to the question. When a given individual dies and disappears from view, what happens to him? He goes to sleep and rests from his labours and forgets his sufferings. If his death be violent or if he has committed suicide his sleep will be disturbed by dreams of his earth life; his apparition or "ghost" may often be accounted for in this way. According to the Society for Psychical Research, ghosts belong to the phenomena of dreamland; sometimes the *agent* and sometimes the *percipient* is dreaming. Mr. F. W. Myers once described a ghost as a "dead man talking in his sleep". The commonest variety, or *stock* ghost, is that of the sailor son who appears to his mother in London, dripping wet, at the same time (verified subsequently) that he was drowned in mid-Atlantic. This kind of ghost is usually accounted for by calling it a telepathic impact happening just *before* the drowning man lost consciousness. This and similar cases are numerous, as anyone may ascertain who will go to the trouble of collecting them. But there is another class of apparitions usually to be found in houses that have the reputation of being haunted owing to a crime having been committed—perhaps a century or more ago. This kind of ghost is called an "astral reflect", and there is reason to think it automatic, depending on the presence or absence of certain electric conditions in the atmosphere. It has a taste for appearing in the "tapestried chamber", the woollen material being a bad conductor and perhaps favourable to electro-magnetic conditions. But some apparitions are *sui generis* and defy all attempts at rational explanation, like tales told by seafaring men. Some of these "yarns" are probably invented, but there is one told in the *Occult Review* some years ago in which the character of the captain who related it is vouched for by the shipowners, a highly-respectable Liverpool firm.[1]

But it is important to remember that these dreams on which the spiritualists rely for evidence are nothing more than dreams of earth life and belong to its final stage. The true spiritual life of the dead person does not begin until he wakes, or is *born* into, globe *e*. Not until then does he discover that he has a body and is surrounded by other people with bodies, just as real—indeed, far more real than he possessed on globe *d*, if the test of reality is density, for there is nothing so dense as the ether. Whether this new body is composed of, or is a modification of, the ether of space, it may be properly called an etherial, or, as St. Paul says, a glorified or resurrection body; a fit habitation for the eternal life which is the reward of the knowledge of Him and the Father who sent Him.

---

[1] "Some Strange Mid-Ocean Visits", *Occult Review*, March, 1906. Rider & Co., London.

Such bodies are, of course, invisible to us at our present stage of evolution, but it is a question how far we are invisible to them or whether their knowledge of us depends on what we call sight. We have a dim, but true, knowledge of things we have not seen nor ever can see. No one has ever seen a proton or electron, but we know that the whole earth and all that it contains, including our own bodies, is an aggregate of protons and electrons. The knowledge of those who have evolved the resurrection body of us who still inhabit globe d may be of the same character, or it may be more direct, arising from a more perfect and quickened sense of apprehension,[1] but, in any case, they see us as we are rather than as we appear, which disposes of the mother and son difficulty alluded to in the preface to this work. The man of sixty has no doubt of his identity with the child of six; he knows that grey hair and wrinkles have only affected his outward appearance; and much in the same way the landscape artist who contemplates his finished picture can recognize in it the broad masses of colour he painted as its foundation. But

---

[1] Hence the visibility in *white* light of our Lord and Moses and Elias in their glorified bodies on the Mount of the Transfiguration.

59

as the new-born child on earth has to adapt himself
to earth conditions, make proper use of his senses,
learn to recognize his parents and his family, learn
to speak, write, etc., so must the new arrival on
globe e learn to adapt himself to his resurrection
body environment. This is so utterly different from
anything we can imagine on globe d that education
itself will take the form, first of learning to recognize the essence of things themselves, and next of
the proper use of symbolism to arrive at secrets of
the universe (those, e.g., in which infinity is a
constant function) that would be otherwise unintel-
ligible. Speech or language will play a very minor
part in the education of globe e children. It will
be regarded as an animal instinct and discouraged
as pertaining to the inferior creation, the more
highly-developed of whom will cease to be "dumb"
animals and begin to acquire the rudiments of
speech. There is no law of Nature to separate
eternally the reciprocal affection of the faithful dog
for his master: that very affection is an important
element in evolution, as every student of the
Mystery of Affinity will acknowledge. But we are
not here concerned with the evolution of the animal
kingdom on the terrestrial chain. The Redemption

of the world through our Lord Jesus Christ includes all animate beings. It is a universal truth, as St. Paul reminds us, that "the *whole creation* groaneth and travailleth in pain together until now, waiting for the adoption, to wit, the redemption of the body."[1] Language will be then recognized for what it is, a medium of deception as well as information. Its place will be taken partly by symbolism and partly by a species of intuitive thought-reading, which, given favourable conditions, can be cultivated like any other faculty. A perfected spiritual body will develop this gift to a degree utterly incomprehensible to us on this earth and make it the normal method of communication, not only with our fellow-men, but, as I have said, also with intelligences far higher than men. To a certain extent this faculty has been developed by occultists here on earth. The writer was once shown a parchment covered with mathematical and astronomical signs to be used as a kind of musical score to establish harmonic relations between human beings and certain planetary "Rectors". The criticism he made on it at the time was that a musical score is useless until instruments have been

---

[1] Rom. viii, 22-3.

invented to interpret the music. Such experiments
are highly dangerous, for, if they could be carried
out, there are evil, as well as good, "higher
intelligences" that might take advantage of them.

At this point it may be asked whether the conditions we have described apply to all men at all
stages of culture and civilization. Death is the fate
of all, savage and civilized. Does the undeveloped
man attain to the spiritual, or resurrection, body
when he is re-born on what we have agreed to call
globe *e*? To give a categorical answer is impossible;
we can only suggest one. A time will come—
it may be ages hence—when the beasts themselves
will be redeemed. They have a certain individuality
here, but they lose it (for the most part) at death:
for every animal that dies or is killed on earth
another is born, immediately, or in a very short
time. The instruments of the Divine Providence
here are known to occultists as the Nature spirits
who preside over the evolution of animals and
plants, and even the law of crystallization in the
mineral kingdom. It is time to examine the nature
of a material and an etheric body, for it is evident
that when St. Paul referred to a "spiritual" body
he meant the latter.

CHAPTER VI

THE ETHERIC BODY

APOLLONIUS of Tyana, having inquired of a Brahmin how can there be a fifth element beside earth, air, fire and water, the Brahmin replied: " There is the ether, which we must regard as the element of which the gods are made, for, just as all mortal creatures inhale the air, so do immortal and divine natures inhale the ether."

Everything we know about the ether points to its being permanent. Matter is only sub-permanent. The "everlasting" hills rise and fall; the changes are slow but inevitable.

> The hills are shadows and they flow
> From form to form and nothing stands.
> They melt like mist, the solid lands
> Like clouds they shape themselves and go.

Of ancient civilizations we find only traces; the

most solid buildings are temporary. Not that the energy that called them into existence goes out of existence; it changes its form and ceases to be available, like milk spilled on the ground, which, though it still exists, ceases to be useful. But, though matter and energy are equivalent, they are not identical, for energy may take a variety of forms. The energy may be that of an electric current, and is then called magnetism, which propels our street cars. Energy is constant in quantity; it changes its form. The moving electrons of which our bodies are composed are surrounded by a magnetic field. It is important to recognize that the ether and its properties are absolutely permanent: there is no irregularity or random motion as there is in the atoms of a gas or solid.

Matter exists not only in the inorganic form of solids, liquids and gases, and in the disintegrated form of electrons and protons, but also as the complex molecules known as protoplasm, which, for some reason or other, has shown itself to be the vehicle of life. Life can take a variety of forms, and every form is characterized by a certain shape. The life of an oak is transmitted to an oak. "To every seed its own body", whether of a man, a bird, a reptile, a fish, or a quadruped. An animal or vegetable body has an undoubted character of its own even to minute detail. And this character is handed down from one generation to another, modified, perhaps, but only slowly, by the age-long process of evolution. At a certain stage in that process conscious mind also enters into relations with it: life and mind use matter for a time and then disappear. We have no right to say they go out of existence, for if they are real things that is quite unlikely. What we know is that life and mind temporarily animate and control matter and then go out of our ken. We know that a body of any shape or of any solid material cannot exist without cohesion which holds the atoms together in that particular shape. Not only is there a matter body, but there is also an ether body, or, as St. Paul expressed it, there is a natural body and a spiritual body.[1] He calls it spiritual because it is characterized by mind, consciousness, memory, affection and other attributes, which he calls the "fruits of the spirit", and distinguishes from the works of

---

[1] I Cor. xv, 44, 45.

the flesh in the "natural" (or soulish χυχικον) body.[1]

The above is taken, for the most part, from Sir Oliver Lodge's "Ether and Reality". It is quite a remarkable example of the reaction of the latest modern scientific thought (1925) from the crass materialism of the last century, as will be seen if we compare it with Professor Tyndall's address to the British Association at Belfast in 1882. But, in spite of the trend of modern science, there still exist valiant survivals like Sir Arthur Keith, who, before the same British Association of amateurs, proved from "scentific" evidence, only the other day, that man could not survive the death of the body; not recognizing that his own opinions on the subject were a survival of the "science" of forty or fifty years ago, and as much out-of-date as phlogiston or the Ptolemaic epicycles in modern astronomy. The question is, "Does man only mature and then die, or is that process but part of a larger destiny?" We cannot deny that, on the answer to this question—did we but know it—all conduct and all values turn. A loose tile from a house-top may destroy the mechanism of thought

---

[1] Gal. v, 19, etc.

and damage irretrievably the workings of an organism.

From Marlboro's eyes the tears of dotage flow,
And swift expires a driveller and a show.

Towards the end of life even Kant's gigantic intellect left him: did it go out of existence? So far as we learn from science, nothing goes out of existence, it only changes its form. It may become inappreciable to our senses and thus *apparently* cease to be. When a moving electron is stopped by some heavy atom getting in the way, as in Professor Ernest Rutherford's bombarding experiments, the electric and magnetic fields, which had previously existed quietly together, now combine into an etheric disturbance, and a *quantum* (or packet of energy) is discharged into space as radiation. But it need not be the visible matter with which we are acquainted. We know from the spectroscope that infra-red and ultra-violet rays exist, for some of these have been photographed and otherwise utilized. It may be that in the not very distant future we may succeed in proving by actual experiment the existence of the etheric body by taking a photograph of one. That once done,

67

further experiments may throw some light on its composition and the nature of its environment. Science has lately been moving at such a rate that it is possible discoveries may be made in quite a reasonable time that will revolutionize our ideas in regard to both the seen and the unseen Universe. At present we do not know what is the nature of an electric charge. We only know it is of two kinds which we call positive and negative, though we might as well call them a and b. But we do know that all matter is made up of these electric charges and that its seeming permanence depends on their equilibrium in the elements in their periodic order. We also know that one element may be changed into another by the addition or subtraction of negative electrons from the positive proton. This looks as if the "dreams" of the alchemists were about to be realized, which, so far, they have not. We can turn gold into a sort of lead called thorium, but we cannot reverse the process.

We must now return to the question of whether a Hottentot or a Bushman will develop a spiritual body when he passes at death to "globe e". Certainly he will have an etheric body, for the ether penetrates the interstices of his material body and is the cause of its shape, and is, moreover, the medium of his sense of touch; for, as we have seen, there can be no real contact between atoms, every one of which is separated from another by an imperceptible cushion of ether. Perhaps the term will be better understood if we call the etheric the "astral body",[1] but whether it is, or is capable of becoming, the true spiritual body in St. Paul's sense of the word, will depend to a great extent on its environment and his own capability. The evolution from the mere colourless "astral" form to the true spiritual body will be only a question of time where the conditions are favourable, and they will be far more favourable than any provided by earth conditions. Here the savage requires to be first coerced and then educated, so far as he is capable of receiving education: there the employment of force in connection with the astral form would be as ridiculous as trying to coerce a shadow. The same applies not only to savages, but lunatics and imbeciles, who are all subject to the "law of death in their mortal bodies", but get their chance afterwards. But here another problem presents

---

[1] The term is used very loosely and is applied indifferently to the body of cohesion or projection.

itself. What will be the fate of the incurably bad and vicious after death? Most of the sins we know are what are called sins of the flesh—murder, theft, adultery, etc., and the wicked and unrepentant man finds himself in a condition where there is no room for their exercise. But if he *loves* sin death does not alter his nature, and he will seek to indulge his evil passions vicariously in the persons of his fellow-sinners on the earth he has left behind. This is the one and only valid argument against Capital Punishment. The murderer is far more dangerous after his execution than before, if we only knew it. Cruel punishments beget crime. The burning alive of witches in the seventeenth century produced a perfect epidemic of witchcraft. It is commonly supposed that the "imaginary" crime of witchcraft became extinct owing to the spread of education. The reply to that is that the establishment of elementary schools has not killed the belief in witchcraft yet in outlying parts of Great Britain and Ireland, and Dr. Franz Hartmann testifies to its existence in the agricultural districts of Germany.[1] What has contributed more than

---

[1] See *The Occult Review* for May, 1906, and reports from time to time in the public Press in English and Continental countries.

anything else to the practical disappearance of witchcraft in the more civilized countries of Europe is the more humane treatment of the old and poor, who are now regarded as objects of pity rather than fear and hatred. This, however, is by the way. There is such a thing as *spiritual* wickedness, and it takes chiefly the form of obsession. One of our Lord's works of mercy on earth was casting out devils. The formulas for exorcism are still retained in certain parts of the Church, though in most cases the necessary faith, in obstinate cases, can only be cultivated through prayer and fasting,[1] and it is so little understood that exorcism is frequently applied to "haunted" houses and even to the strange phenomenon of the "poltergeist", when, though the so-called devil smashes crockery, rarely does any serious harm to human beings. The wretched victims of obsession, now mostly confined in lunatic asylums, exhibit the most repulsive forms of mania, from homicide to gross indecency, and, including both sadism and masochism, are not altogether *innocent* victims, for they have indulged in evil thoughts and, so to

---

[1] Mark ix, 29.

speak, voluntarily opened their doors to the intruders. Once established in the personality, their host becomes as wax in their hands.

In taking leave of this unpleasant subject I have only to add that exorcism would be far more successful if the exorcists themselves did not yield to fear but always remembered their own dignity as human beings in the flesh, which our Lord came to sanctify by taking flesh unto Himself.

CHAPTER VII

THE LINKING OF THIS CHAIN WITH A HIGHER

IN discussing the Future of Man I must proceed warily. Certain occult "secrets" I consider myself at liberty to reveal, and have revealed up to a point, but others I am not, even when I have discovered them unaided. Some of these I shall deal with under the heading of Symbiosis, and if anyone chooses to read between the lines and learn anything for himself I am not responsible, for I have taken no oath and am violating no confidence. So far I have said nothing of the relations of the dead to the living, except to try and prove that the séance-room "spirits" are not really *dead* people, and also that the phenomenon of obsession is due to certain exceptionally wicked spirits among those who have departed. But the large majority are far from being wicked, having taken advantage of the new conditions to repent sincerely, like the Publican in the Parable, of the sins they committed in the flesh and are bringing forth "fruits meet for repentance",

73

while a certain number, though a minority, might even be called saints. A saint does not mean an exceptionally religious person, or one by whose relics miracles are performed. In the infant Church the term included all Christians who had died in the Faith, and the "Communion of Saints" was the privilege of all, both here and of those who had "fallen asleep in Jesus". Our duty to them was to pray that they might rest in peace until the time came for their awaking to the resurrection life. In the Holy Orthodox Churches of the East, where the original traditions are preserved, it is the custom to pray for our deceased friends for forty days and to seek their prayers for ourselves ever afterwards. Forty days is probably a rough average: in cases of a long and wasting illness this period of rest may be much longer; but for the martyrs whose sufferings came to an end suddenly and the penitent thief on the Cross the "seventh age of man" had for its duration probably the time it takes to recover from a fainting fit. The penitent thief whose legs were broken on Good Friday awoke probably on Holy Saturday, or at least met his Lord, as promised, on Easter Day. For those who have attained the resurrection body there is no more death (except the *second* death of the wicked, Rev. xx, 15), but not until the Judgment Day are "all tears wiped away". The incessant struggle in the War with the Prince of this World, and their apparent failure to destroy his works and deliver mankind from his machinations, must be a source of bitter grief to the redeemed. Their suffering at the delay of the Final Judgment must at times be acute.

It is true they are fighting in this age-long Holy War under the leadership of Angels and Archangels and all the company of Heaven, but they are the private soldiers who have to do the actual fighting. The responsibility of conducting the War rests with their Prince and His officers. Now what is the nature of this War in which we fight not with carnal weapons but against Powers and Principalities and spiritual wickedness in the supercelestial regions?[1] A spiritual war is a war of ideas. The world is ruled by ideas, and often wrong and false ones. As we have seen, the institution of speech and writing has contributed very largely to this. False religions, false science and degraded art spring from this imperfect

---

[1] Eph. vi, 12. ἐν τοῖς ἐπουρανίοις

medium of thought. But nothing false can last for long; its falsity is discovered sooner or later, and yet may give way to other ideas, perhaps equally false. The labours of those who endeavour to substitute true ones resemble those of Sisyphus. And yet the thought of any particular age or period is a collective product. To those in touch, even here, with the changes which have occurred all over the world within the last very few years in financial and industrial groupings it is impossible to avoid the conviction that if civilization is to be saved Society must change its basis from one of competition to the saner one of co-operation.

This, indeed, is the great spiritual task which it is now the duty of those who have passed on to undertake. How shall they change the ideas of the nineteenth century so firmly rooted in the minds of thousands of people and adapt them to the new conditions? It is in sleep that ideas are often changed, for sleep is often the medium chosen to impart spiritual knowledge. The impression on the subconscious mind finds it way into the brain, where it takes shape and becomes an idea, a part of our mental furniture, to be worked out in our waking-hours. In a suitable soil the seed, once implanted, grows; the idea is imparted to others, sometimes with revolutionary effect. This is no new task. Society must always rest on some fundamental instinct. In Feudal Europe it rested on a military basis; the desire for power rather than the desire for possession. This had to be destroyed to make way for a new era. A spirit fatal to the whole system of the Middle Ages lay in John Ball's popular rhyme: "When Adam delved and Eve span, who was then the gentleman?" Moreover, the military and religious orders tended to breed themselves out of existence by war and the religious by celibacy. The same fate must overtake the new plutocracy with its ideals of sexual promiscuity (called freedom to divorce) tempered with birth control. These are the dangers with which modern society is threatened: they are dangers of its *spirit*, and they can only be combatted by spiritual influences. Here, as in many other ways, the Church on earth can co-operate with those who have gone before if we only care to avail ourselves of a privilege secured to us by the Creed, belief in the Communion of Saints, a true spiritual communion resting on faith and requiring the intervention of no "mediums" as in the false one of necromancy.

But it is time to consider another question. Is life in the next world or psychic centre to which we are attracted after the death of the material body eternal, or, if there is birth on "globe e", is there anything corresponding to death? No, but there is something corresponding to removal which takes the form of promotion from the ranks to the position of officers, and of this we shall treat under the heading of symbiosis and meta-symbiosis.

.   .   .   .   .

No competent biologist will deny that symbiosis or biological reciprocity of organisms on any given planet—our earth for instance—has far-reaching reactions upon the course of evolution. Some examples of this inter-dependence will be familiar to all. We all know that animal life is in the last resort dependent on plants for food, for even the carnivorous prey on the herbivorous animals. Many micro-organisms assist plant life by changing dead parts of animals or plants into valuable plant food. Again, the production by animals of the carbonic acid essential to planet life is another example of reciprocity. The partnership between the algæ and the sponges, whereby the former supply the latter with oxygen while using for food the carbonic di-oxide given off by the sponge tissues, is another example taken from a long list, and proves that mutual service on the part of individual organisms is a cardinal factor in the evolution of living things. Chemical compounds containing carbon hydrogen and oxygen with their unique properties, especially of forming water and carbonic acid, seem to envisage a principle applying not only to material life but to life in all conditions and at all stages of evolution. If there is a material symbiosis at the foundation of life here on this planet, may there not be something corresponding—what I may perhaps call a *meta-symbiosis*—or co-operation of effort for mutual help applying to other regions in which life manifests itself? To take only one instance, the place of respiratory exchange has its analogy in meta-symbiosis in the amount and quality of the energy liberated by spiritual effort—that, for example, which enabled one servant to turn into ten the talent entrusted to him, and the other into only five. This is known to theologians as "The Treasury of Merit" on which all can draw for their benefit, though it has nothing to do with the so-called "imputed" merits that are an element in the scheme of salvation, but have reference to benefits of quite another kind.

I have said in Chapter V that the terrestrial chain becomes linked with another at the point we have called globe *e* ruled by an exalted intelligence known as a *Principality* of Light. Both belong to the region called by the Jews the *Third* Heaven[1] to distinguish it from the atmosphere and the location of the sun, moon, and stars, and by the Catholic Church the place where the saints enjoy the Beatific Vision. The connection is a mysterious one, on which I am unwilling to dogmatize, but it is supposed to have a bearing on the Second Advent when, as St. Jude says, quoting from the Book of Enoch:

> " Behold the Lord comes with myriads of
> His Holy ones
> " To execute judgement upon all", etc.[2]

It is not generally known that our sun is a double star. As its companion is a dark body and has consequently never been observed, the idea would

---

[1] 2 Cor. xii, 2.
[2] E. of Judas. Dr. Moffatt's Translation.

be laughed at by the very competent astronomers on the staff at Greenwich, though we may at any time read in the newspapers the discovery of a new star nearer than *proxima* in Centaur—perhaps this time in the Northern Hemisphere. It is probably smaller than the sun, though many times larger than Jupiter, and it is not yet near enough to shine with reflected light. When discovered, it will be announced as a new planet far more remote than Neptune, thus defying Bode's "law" of periodic orbital proportion of distances. We know that the stability of our solar system depends on attraction, and it has been somewhat hastily assumed that it is a universal law which applies throughout space. But attraction and repulsion are, in fact, alternate.

At a certain small distance which we call contact, repulsion (say, between two lumps of iron) succeeds attraction, and can only be overcome by the process called welding, when the *repulsion* of contact is succeeded by the molecular *attraction* called cohesion. At a smaller distance we get atomic repulsion, and at a smaller still we have the attraction of the proton for the electron and the repulsion of the electrons for each other. When we turn from atomic and molecular to astronomical distances we find in our solar system that attraction in the form of gravitation prevails as far as the planet Neptune, and probably many times farther, but if the law of alternation holds good we should expect the fixed stars to repel one another. Astronomical distances are calculated by light velocity. The light distance of Neptune from the sun is somewhere about four *hours*, whereas the nearest fixed star is separated from us by a little more than three light *years*. What follows?

If there are astronomers in Sirius, or Vega in the constellation of the Lyre, separated from us by about twenty-one light years, a sudden discovery will be made one day that our sun is a double star. Assuming that their telescopes are as good as, but no better than, ours, they will not perceive that this interesting phenomenon has been purchased at the price of the destruction of our solar system, for they are too far away to know if such a thing exists.

About ten or fifteen years ago we witnessed a somewhat similar catastrophe. A small star in the constellation Perseus suddenly blazed up into one of the first magnitude. It lasted about three weeks and then subsided into its original size of the sixth. As the phenomenon actually took place when

Elizabeth was on the English throne, it was observed curiously but soon forgotten. For all that, it was a misfortune for anyone who might be living there in the Sixteenth Century, or, indeed, anywhere in the neighbourhood of the fire.

We read of these things, but attach less importance to them in education than the Fire of London in 1666, and never dream that such things may happen to us. We hear in church the words of St. Paul: " Behold I shew you a mystery, We shall not all die but we shall all be changed in a moment, in the twinkling of an eye," etc.,[1] and wonder if the last trumpet will be made of Birmingham brass and blown by an apparent young woman in a white dress with a pair of goose-wings attached to her shoulder-blades. If we could only rid ourselves of the idea that St. Paul was not only not a fool, but a poet and a master of occult science into the bargain, we should not talk like fools ourselves, and perhaps incline to think over his words.

A time will certainly come (sooner, perhaps, than is generally supposed) when, owing to an astronomical catastrophe, the earth will become incandescent vapour, and every living thing on it

---

[1] 1 Cor. xv, 51, etc.

83

suddenly exchange its material for an etheric body, so suddenly that it will take some time to get used to the difference. But they will know they are being judged, and even judging themselves, for thoughts and deeds committed in the body, and many will learn for the first time what righteousness (or justice δικαιοσύνη) is and what it implies when translated into terms of conduct.

But we have travelled a long way from the terrestrial chain and its linking up with another. The fact is, a certain number of the redeemed will have rendered themselves by faithful service fit for archangelic functions. In the remote past certain Heavenly beings "kept not their first estate" but, under the leadership of a Principality, or planetary Rector, rebelled against God's purpose when He created man. Accordingly, their places had to be filled up, and it is the opinion of several theologians that, in the councils of the Most High, that destiny was reserved for human beings. Now what is the nature of the archangels? As living creatures, they cannot be pure spirit but must have a body of some kind. It is not etheric but *super etheric,* or not individualized in the human sense of the word, but only in so far as they represent groups

of human activity. They stand for groups of men
—ethnic, civic, scientific, or any other group in
which men associate themselves for a purpose.
Their work on earth is often impeded by Satan,
who endeavours to substitute an archangel of darkness for one of light—Mammon, Beelzebub, etc.,
in the case of nations, and other false "gods" to
degrade art and science.[1] The celestial ranks have
been depleted by the rebellion and they would wel-
come recruits drawn from mankind. This function
is hinted at in the Parable of the Talents. "Be thou
ruler over ten or five *cities*" seems to point to it
clearly. Also, the presumption of the Apostles
James and John was met by the answer of our Lord
that the desired places were received by the Father
for those "to whom they have been destined"[2]
This linking of the two chains belongs to the higher

[1] Beelzebub has been called the "god of flies". Disease germs
would be more correct. The life of these microscopic creatures which
are the cause of zymotic disease, and, indeed, all forms of parasitic
life, are determined by lunar influences and are consequently under
the control of the Lord of the Eighth Sphere. This is well known
to those who practice evil magic or sorcery. Mammon (whose name
is derived from the Syriac word for riches) is one of the "rulers of
the darkness of this world" (Eph. vi, 12). He is the god of barriers
and presides over all those influences which are begotten of ignorance,
prejudice, and fear. It is for this reason that he is supposed to be
connected with material wealth as constituting a false standard of
worth and dignity.
[2] Matt. xx, 23.

arcana of occultism. So far as I know, it has only been revealed to the occult fraternity of the ——, and I am very grateful to the two brothers who have informed me of it, and attached no restrictions on my making use of the information.

Here I come to the end of my tether. It is not for me, or any mortal, to endeavour to penetrate the dread secrets of the "Final Assize". They are of a spiritual character, and the Judgement "Day" should no more be taken literally than the six days of Creation or the seventh, when God "rested from His labours" and has been resting ever since. We learn that the Father judgeth no man but hath committed all judgement unto the Son,[1] who will return with ten thousand of His saints to judge both the quick and the dead. The next chapter will be devoted to gathering up the threads of my argument.

---

[1] John v, 22.

CHAPTER VIII

A CHANGING WEB

Geburt und grab
Ein wechselnd Weben
Ein glühend Leben,
So schaf'ich am sausenden Webstühl der Zeit
Und wirke der Gottheit lebendiges Kleid.[1]—Goethe's *Faust*.

OCCULT Science consists in the penetration of the Seven Great Mysteries, and the real secrets which are so jealously guarded are not the same kind of secrets which I am supposed to have partially revealed in this work. The penetration is of a spiritual nature, and, as all spirit must have a body, the body must consist of facts, some of which may, and others may not, be imparted. Behind every fact there is a spiritual perception which is the essence of the knowledge and gives it validity. Every fact revealed is a seed. It may fall on stony ground, in which case it remains merely a seed, and food for the fowls of the air. It may fall

---

[1] Birth and Death, a changing web, a glowing life. Thus do I work at the humming loom of Time and fashion the living garment of God.

among thorns and be perverted from its true purpose, or it may fall on good ground and bear spiritual fruit in the shape of faith. Since the Great War the reality and value of the external world, and the collective soul of a people, has borne fruit in Germany in a new Relativism of a transcendental character in the person of a new philosopher, Herr O. Spengler,[1] who has been at pains to trace the downfall of the political system, in which Germany has placed her faith for nearly two generations, to a too narrow view of history and the part which every nation, European and Asiatic, must play in Weltpolitik.

The facts I have revealed about Birth and Death will probably be rejected with ridicule by many people, who will say: " How should he know more than another?" But there are other readers to whom they will appeal in the sense that a particular movement in a symphony is perceived to be part of an organic whole in which it has its place and will fill no other.

I examined first the pretensions of the people who profess to find a key to the solution through

[1] Der Untergang de Abendlandes. 2 Vols. 1920-1922. English Translation, 1926-1928.

"mediums", and I claim to have proved that the revelations are nothing more than dreams of the deceased about their former earth life. From that I proceeded to discuss modern Theosophy and its pseudo-occultism; and then endeavoured to show that for the evolution of spiritual man in an etheric, or spiritual, body the symbolism we call speech and language must give way to another kind of symbolism less capable of being perverted to the propagation of falsehood by the Father of lies who is the Prince of this world, and whose government is founded on the systematic deception required to blind men's eyes to their true interests. Whether his ingenuity will be equal to cope with the new symbolism, and the intuition on which it will be founded, is doubtful. His resources are tremendous, but we shall have the help of the higher intelligences who, under the leadership of the lawful Prince, are pledged to destroy the Devil and all his works. When they succeed—and they must finally succeed: it is only a question of time —the astronomic catastrophe at which I have hinted will take place. The etheric bodies of the wicked will be drawn irresistibly into the vortex of the Eighth Sphere where their energy will be converted into radiation which is a half-way stage between ether and matter. Radiation tends to spread to the confines of the universe. It is emitted and absorbed in *quanta*, or packets of energy; it carries momentum and exerts pressure. There must be some deep meaning in the speed at which lights travels; no greater speed seems possible. In that speed and in the newly-presented puzzles about the connection between ether and matter and the nature of radiation—problems which are beginning to take definite shapes—we are down among the foundations of material being, and possibly the creation of a new solar system in some unimaginable depths of space. In ending our inquiry into the Mystery of Birth and Death, we cannot do better than quote the words of Sir Oliver Lodge at the conclusion of his "Ether and Reality":

" Confronted with a majestic view of Reality, we—like those other explorers on their first view of the Pacific Ocean—have

" ' Looked at each other with a wild surmise,
    Silent upon a peak in Darien.' "

APPENDIX

THAT speech and writing should continue to be the chief medium of communication between rational creatures is unthinkable, for it carries with it the constant danger of being deceived, and is in fact the chief weapon of the Prince of this world who is the Father of lies. What is called Public Opinion is a manufactured article, and "government of the people for the people by the people" a tragic farce. The chief force of the modern Press lies in its power to intensify any mental disease prevalent in the masses. They dislike thinking or any sustained effort, but the Press saves them the trouble by providing pictures and head-lines. It has been said that if people were told every day that the moon was made of green cheese they would in time come to believe it. They do come to believe that Huggins's Whisky or Buggins's Cigarettes are the best, merely because the proprietors of those articles tell them they are every day. At this time of writing a leading journal is making enormous profits by inserting *comic* pictures of chauffeurs persuading the owners of motor-cars to use a particular kind of oil and refuse all others. The contempt shown for their readers almost passes belief. It is not long ago that a millionaire proprietor of several newspapers aspired to the office of Prime Minister by threatening with dismissal certain members of the Government who would not dance to his tune with " A.B. or C.M.G. must go". But they not only blackmail politicians, but suppress truths that should be told in the public interest and substitute lies for them by orders to their foreign correspondents. A flagrant example of this is given in Mr. H. W. Nevinson's book, "Last Changes and Chances":

> Orders were received from England by certain of the correspondents to represent the Germans as being fat and prosperous, and, as ordered, the information was supplied. I read an account of the wealth and luxury of Cologne, the sleek and rosy children of the poor two days afterwards in the correspondent's paper.[1]

This abuse of power is not confined to the secular

---

[1] Quoted by Mr. H. W. Nevinson from "Disenchantment", by C. E. Montague, pp. 151-176, First Edition.

but applies also to the "religious" Press, which is quite as unscrupulous. Formerly, burning alive was the popular method of suppressing inconvenient opinions, but it has been discovered that the boycott is a much more effectual weapon nowadays. The writer knows a case in which the Editor of an Anglo-Catholic weekly has been forbidden not only to print any letters he may send to that newspaper, but also to take no notice of anything he may say or write elsewhere. When we consider how the gift of language has been abused and made to subserve the vilest ends we shall no longer wonder that occult science teaches that it came from the lunar pitris or angels of darkness from the Eighth Sphere. *Timeo Danaos et dona ferentes.* It will have to be superseded by an intuitive faculty of the nature of the earlier evolved gift of instinct and analogous to the musical faculty where beauty will come into the inheritance of logic, and a hitherto unknown symbolism be established in the interests of spiritual truth and the avoidance of falsehood in all departments of human activity. In this, and in this way only, shall we come to recognize that our Lord is the Way, the Truth, and the Life, and that no man cometh to the Father but by Him.

"THE FOURTH MYSTERY"

Since the above was written, the Swarthmore Lecture on "Science and the Unseen World" for 1929, by the eminent astronomer, Prof. A. S. Eddington, F.R.S., has been published. The Professor, who is a member of the "Society of Friends", was "moved by the Spirit" to write as follows:

" We have the same desire as of old to get to the bottom of things, but the ideal of what constitutes a scientific explanation has changed almost beyond recognition. And if to-day you ask a physicist what he has finally made out the ether or the electron to be . . . he will point to a number of symbols and a set of mathematical equations which they satisfy. What do the symbols stand for? The mysterious reply is given that physics is indifferent to that; it has no means of probing beneath the symbolism. To understand the phenomena of the physical world it is necessary to know the equations which the symbols obey but not the nature of that which is being symbolised." And again: " We all share the strange delusion that a lump of matter is something whose general nature is easily comprehensible, whereas the nature of the human spirit is unfathomable. . . . It is just because we have a real and not merely a symbolic knowledge of our own nature that our nature seems so mysterious. In comparing the certainty of things spiritual and things temporal, let us not forget this: Mind is the first and most direct thing in our experience; *all else is remote inference.*"

One last quotation:

"Natural law is not applicable to the unseen world behind the symbols, because it is unadapted to anything except symbols, *and its perfection is a perfection of symbolic linkage.* You cannot apply such a scheme to the parts of our personality that are not measurable by symbols any more than you can extract the square root of a sonnet."

The Swarthmore Lecture represents the latest results of the best scientific thought by one of the boldest thinkers with a European reputation for knowledge and clarity of expression. The Swarthmore Lecture is published at one and sixpence and should be read by every reader of this book and all who are interested in the trend of modern thought.

THE END

www.ingramcontent.com/pod-product-compliance
Lightning Source LLC
LaVergne TN
LVHW011408080426
835511LV00005B/434